ANIMALS
ANIMALS

ELEPHANTS

BY MARTIN SCHWABACHER

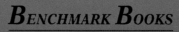

BENCHMARK BOOKS

MARSHALL CAVENDISH
NEW YORK

Series Consultant: James Doherty
General Curator
Bronx Zoo, New York

Benchmark Books
Marshall Cavendish Corporation
99 White Plains Road
Tarrytown, NY 10591-9001

Library of Congress Cataloging-in-Publication data:
Schwabacher, Martin
Elephants / Martin Schwabacher.
p. cm.
Includes bibliographical references and index.
Summary: Describes the physical characteristics and behavior of elephants, their family groups, food habits, and threats
to their existence.
ISBN 0-7614-1168-2
1. Elephants–Juvenile literature. [1. Elephants.] I. Title.
QL737.P98   S396   2000
599.67–dc21   00-024277

Cover photo: *Animals, Animals* / M. Colbeck.

All photographs are used by permission and through the courtesy of *Animals, Animals:* Anthony Banister, 4, 19; Mickey
Gibson, 7; Ken Cole, 9; Anup Shah, 14 (top left); Roger De La Harpe, 14 (bottom left); Ralph Reinhold, 15; A. and M.
Shah, 18; Betty H. Press, 20; A. Desai, 23; Friedrich Von Horsten, 25; D. Allan Photography, M. Colbeck, 29, 26. 32, 34;
Gerald Lacz, 30; Richard Sobol, 35; J and B Photographers, 36; Bruce Davidson, 38, 39; S. Turner, 40, 41;
Francois Savigny 43.

Printed in China

3 5 6 4

CONTENTS

1
INTRODUCING ELEPHANTS

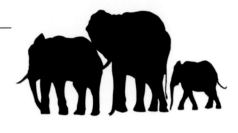

Elephants are the world's biggest land animals. A full-grown elephant towers 10 feet (3 meters) at the shoulder and weighs 6 tons—that's as much as a school bus! Like people, elephants are *mammals*: intelligent, warm-blooded, hairy creatures that give birth to live babies.

The tough, wrinkly skin of an elephant is over an inch thick and weighs a ton all by itself. Elephants like to cover their skin with mud to keep off bugs, stay cool, and prevent sunburn. They also flap their big, floppy ears to keep cool in the hot sun.

THESE AFRICAN ELEPHANTS ARE ENJOYING A MUD BATH.

Some elephants have two giant front teeth called *tusks* that jut out several feet. They use these tusks to dig holes, wrestle, and tear bark off trees.

In place of a nose, elephants have a *trunk*. This long, flexible tube of muscle serves as an arm, hand, nose, trumpet, water hose, and snorkel, all in one. By pinching together the fingerlike tips of their trunks, they can pluck a single blade of grass. Using their trunks like a giant straw, elephants can suck up a gallon of water, and then spray it into their mouth or onto their back to take a shower. They can also blow their trunks like trumpets, whistle, or stomp on them to make funny sounds.

THE AFRICAN ELEPHANT IS THE LARGEST LAND ANIMAL. THE ASIAN ELEPHANT IS A LITTLE SMALLER. BOTH ARE MANY TIMES LARGER THAN HUMAN BEINGS.

AN ELEPHANT'S TUSKS GROW ALL ITS LIFE. BOTH MALE AND FEMALE AFRICAN ELEPHANTS HAVE TUSKS. BUT ONLY MALE ASIAN ELEPHANTS HAVE TUSKS. HOW OLD DO YOU THINK THIS ASIAN ELEPHANT IS?

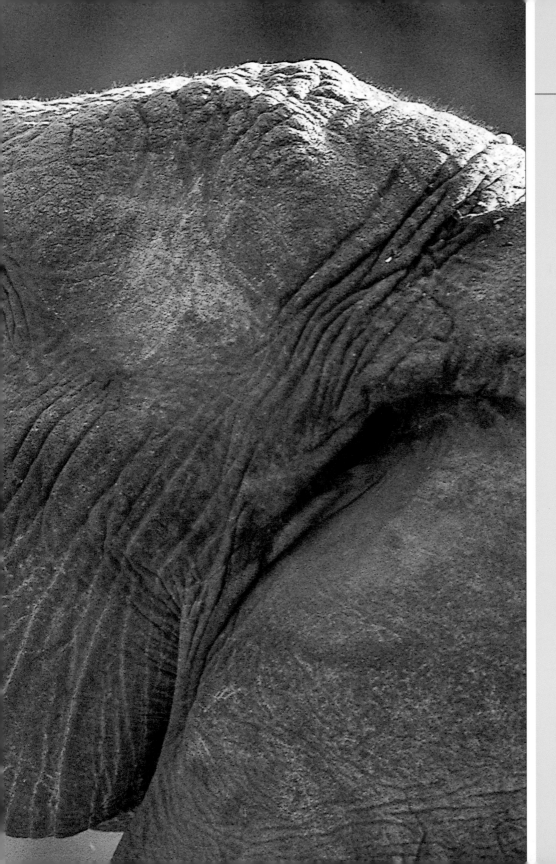

ELEPHANTS USE
THEIR TRUNKS
TO SUCK UP
WATER AND
THEN SPRAY
IT INTO THEIR
MOUTHS.

9

WOOLLY MAMMOTHS LIVED IN EUROPE, ASIA, AND SOUTH AMERICA. THEIR BODIES HAVE BEEN FOUND BURIED IN THE FAR NORTH, UNCHANGED AFTER THOUSANDS OF YEARS. IN 1999, A FROZEN MAMMOTH WAS CARRIED AWAY BY HELICOPTER FOR STUDY. SCIENTISTS MAY TRY TO CLONE A LIVE MAMMOTH FROM ITS CELLS, MUCH AS DINOSAURS WERE CLONED IN THE MOVIE **JURASSIC PARK.**

Elephants have larger brains than any other land animal, including humans. Unlike most other animals, elephants use tools. They will grab a stick to scratch a hard-to-reach itch or throw heavy objects onto a branch to bend it down within reach. Elephants can figure out how to open doors, turn on faucets, and open locks. One elephant not only unchained its legs but put the chain back to hide what it had done! They also have great memories and can remember the path to a water hole they haven't visited in years.

Millions of years ago, there were as many as thirty kinds, or *species*, of elephants. The first elephant-like creature lived fifty million years ago and was the size of a pig. A recent close relative to the elephant was the huge *woolly mammoth*, which had long fur and lived during the last ice age. People hunted mammoths until about ten thousand years ago, when the last ones died. Today, the elephant's nearest relatives are the blubbery *dugong*, or sea cow, which lives in rivers and coastal waters, and the *hyrax*, which is found in trees or rocky areas.

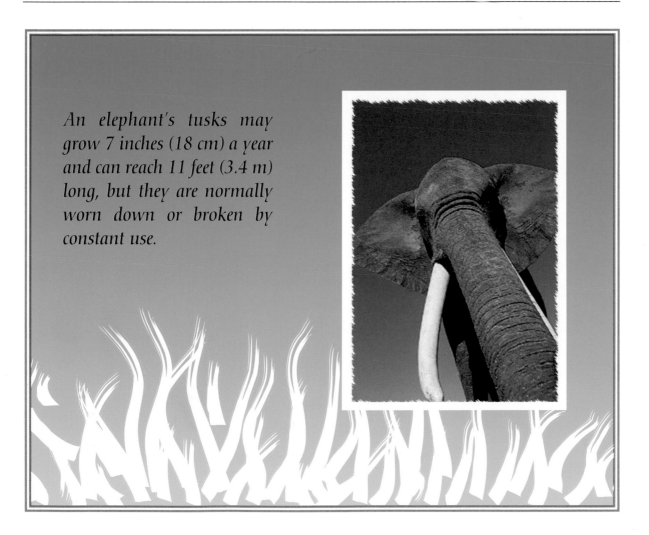

An elephant's tusks may grow 7 inches (18 cm) a year and can reach 11 feet (3.4 m) long, but they are normally worn down or broken by constant use.

2
THE ELEPHANT FAMILY

There are two species of elephants living today: the African and the Asian. African elephants are bigger and have larger ears, more wrinkled skin, and two "fingers" on the end of their trunk. Asian elephants are smaller. They have just one "finger" and a hump on their fore-head. Asian elephants are easier to train; many work in forests hauling lumber.

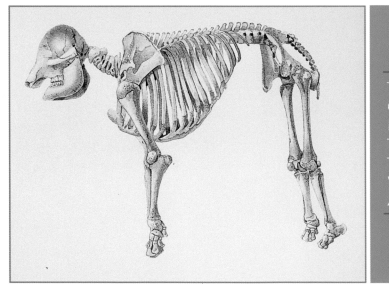

THIS IS THE SKELETON OF AN ASIAN ELEPHANT. NOTICE THE BONE IN THE FRONT OF ITS SKULL. THIS IS THE BONE TO WHICH THE TRUNK ATTACHES.

ASIAN ELEPHANT

AFRICAN ELEPHANT

(TOP) AFRICAN ELEPHANTS HAVE TWO "FINGERS" ON THEIR TRUNKS. (BOTTOM) ASIAN ELEPHANTS HAVE ONLY ONE.

Elephants have adapted to life in many environments. They live in grasslands, forests, marshes, deserts, and mountains. Elephants can go almost anywhere. Some have swum for miles to distant islands, holding their trunks above the water like snorkels to breathe.

Wherever they live, elephants need a lot of space. They crush trees and trample plants when they eat, so they have to keep moving to find more.

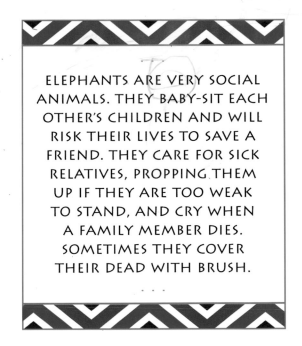

ELEPHANTS ARE VERY SOCIAL ANIMALS. THEY BABY-SIT EACH OTHER'S CHILDREN AND WILL RISK THEIR LIVES TO SAVE A FRIEND. THEY CARE FOR SICK RELATIVES, PROPPING THEM UP IF THEY ARE TOO WEAK TO STAND, AND CRY WHEN A FAMILY MEMBER DIES. SOMETIMES THEY COVER THEIR DEAD WITH BRUSH.

. . .

13

ELEPHANTS CAN LIVE IN MANY DIFFERENT ENVIRONMENTS. THEY ARE FOUND IN FORESTS, LIKE THESE ASIAN ELEPHANTS IN INDIA (UPPER LEFT). THEY ARE ALSO FOUND IN DESERTS , LIKE THESE ELEPHANTS IN NAMIBIA (LOWER LEFT) AND IN GRASSLANDS, LIKE THIS ELEPHANT IN TANZANIA (ABOVE).

15

Elephants may travel 3,000 to 6,000 miles (4,800 to 9,700 kilometers) a year looking for food, the longest migration of any land mammal.

Elephants travel in *herds* led by the oldest female. She knows where to find food and water and how to protect the herd from enemies. Each herd is a family of two to twenty related females and their young. Males travel alone or with other males. They visit the herd to mate and defend the young. Otherwise, they leave the females to run the family.

When members of the herd meet, they rub against each other, sniff and touch each other's trunks, and put them in each other's mouths. They also communicate with each other in trumpet blasts, grunts, growls, rumbles, purrs, and squeals.

Elephants make a rumbling sound so low-pitched that people cannot hear it. But if you touch an elephant, you can feel these vibrations. These ultra-low sounds travel for miles, and elephants may use them to keep in touch with other herds.

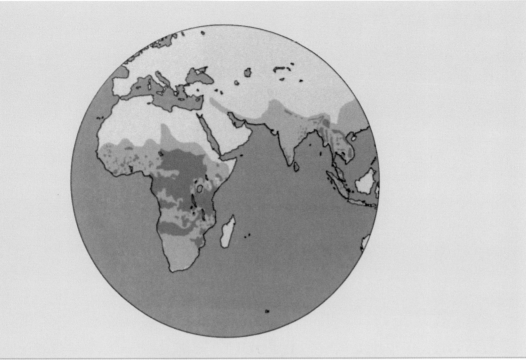

THEN & NOW

This map shows the past and present habitats of African and Asian elephants. Notice how their habitat has grown smaller.

PAST HABITAT

PRESENT HABITAT

ELEPHANTS HAVE DISAPPEARED FROM

The Middle East, Pakistan, China, Java, South Africa, and parts of east Africa

SCATTERED POPULATIONS REMAIN IN

India, Southeast Asia, and most of west Africa

ELEPHANTS ARE OFTEN SEEN TOUCHING EACH OTHER WITH THEIR TRUNKS. EACH TOUCH MEANS SOMETHING DIFFERENT. HERE, ONE ELEPHANT IS SHOWING ITS DOMINANCE BY WRAPPING ITS TRUNK AROUND THE OTHER ELEPHANT.

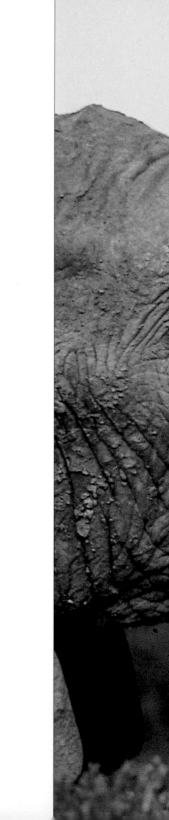

Young elephants often hold their mother's tail with their trunk as they walk, like a human child holding its mother's hand.

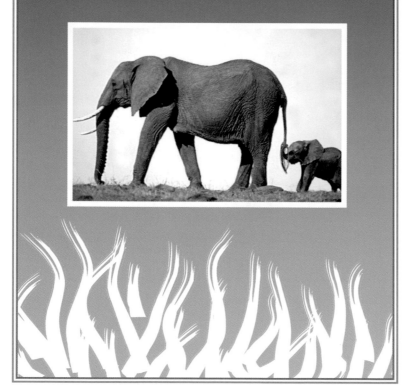

3
ELEPHANT APPETITES

It takes 300 pounds (136 kilograms) of food a day to feed an elephant. Elephants need so much food that they spend sixteen hours a day eating. (Luckily, they need just two to four hours sleep!) Elephants walk up to 40 miles (64 kilometers) a day searching for food. Once a day, they return to a water hole where they may drink as much as 50 gallons (190 liters) of water—enough to fill a bathtub.

Elephants will kill a lion if one attacks them. They can stomp other

THIS ELEPHANT HERD IN KENYA IS TRAVELING IN SEARCH OF FOOD AND WATER. THE LARGE ELEPHANT IN THE FOREGROUND IS THEIR LEADER, THE DOMINANT FEMALE.

animals to death, gore them, or knock them senseless with a blow from their powerful trunk. But elephants are not hunters. They are *herbivores*, peaceful animals that eat only plants.

Elephants eat grass, leaves, roots, bark, buds, fruits, and tree branches. They dig up roots with their tusks and pluck leaves from the treetops with their trunks. Standing on its hind legs, an elephant can reach higher than a giraffe can! A hungry elephant can also rip off a whole branch or knock down an entire tree.

Like all animals, elephants need salt. In Kenya, in east Africa, there is a cave 525 feet (160 m) long dug by elephants scraping salt out of a hillside with their tusks.

ELEPHANTS LOVE SALT SO MUCH THAT THEY WILL DIG LARGE HOLES WITH THEIR TUSKS TO UNCOVER IT. HOW LONG DO YOU THINK IT TOOK THIS YOUNG ASIAN ELEPHANT TO DIG THIS HOLE?

SOMETIMES, ELEPHANTS RIP
THE BARK OFF TREES TO EAT.
OTHER TIMES, THEY USE
THEIR INCREDIBLE STRENGTH
TO KNOCK DOWN AND EAT
AN ENTIRE TREE.

THIS ELEPHANT
WILL STOP AT
NOTHING TO GET
A LEAFY SNACK.

Other animals follow elephants to eat from the trees they knock over. Birds ride on their backs or follow behind, snapping up insects the elephants stir up. Small animals and beetles find seeds in their dung. Elephants also dig water holes from which other animals drink.

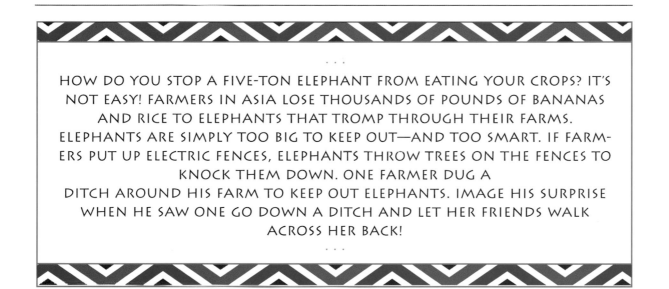

. . .

HOW DO YOU STOP A FIVE-TON ELEPHANT FROM EATING YOUR CROPS? IT'S NOT EASY! FARMERS IN ASIA LOSE THOUSANDS OF POUNDS OF BANANAS AND RICE TO ELEPHANTS THAT TROMP THROUGH THEIR FARMS. ELEPHANTS ARE SIMPLY TOO BIG TO KEEP OUT—AND TOO SMART. IF FARMERS PUT UP ELECTRIC FENCES, ELEPHANTS THROW TREES ON THE FENCES TO KNOCK THEM DOWN. ONE FARMER DUG A DITCH AROUND HIS FARM TO KEEP OUT ELEPHANTS. IMAGE HIS SURPRISE WHEN HE SAW ONE GO DOWN A DITCH AND LET HER FRIENDS WALK ACROSS HER BACK!

. . .

4
THE LIFE OF AN ELEPHANT

When a baby elephant is born, it already stands 3 feet (1 meter) tall at the shoulder and weighs about 250 pounds (110 kilograms)—as much as a pro wrestler! The baby elephant gains pounds every day. Even though it starts grazing after just a few weeks, it will keep drinking its mother's milk for two to four years. By the age of five, the young elephant weighs over 1,000 pounds (450 kilograms). Unlike most animals, which stop growing when they become adults, an elephant keeps getting bigger and bigger all its life. Male elephants wrestle each other with

A NEWBORN AFRICAN ELEPHANT HIDES BEHIND ITS MOTHER. ALREADY THE CALF WEIGHS OVER 200 POUNDS (90 KG)!

ELEPHANT CALVES CAN BE VERY PLAYFUL—
JUST LIKE HUMAN CHILDREN.

their tusks to find out who is the strongest. Only the biggest and strongest males mate with the females. Males often do not get to mate until age thirty, while females are usually mothers by fifteen.

It takes twenty to twenty–two months for a female to give birth after mating. No other animal stays pregnant for such a long time. That's close to two years —more than twice as long as a person is pregnant.

Elephants usually live between forty–five and sixty years. They may lose and regrow their molar teeth six times during their life. When their last set of teeth wears out, elephants can no longer chew food, and they die.

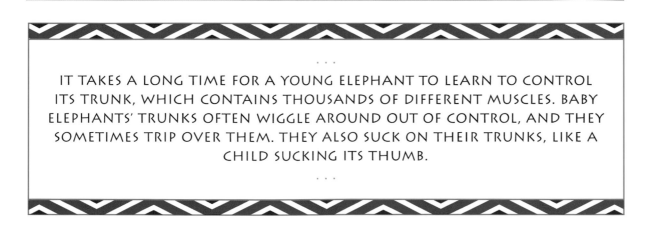

. . .

IT TAKES A LONG TIME FOR A YOUNG ELEPHANT TO LEARN TO CONTROL ITS TRUNK, WHICH CONTAINS THOUSANDS OF DIFFERENT MUSCLES. BABY ELEPHANTS' TRUNKS OFTEN WIGGLE AROUND OUT OF CONTROL, AND THEY SOMETIMES TRIP OVER THEM. THEY ALSO SUCK ON THEIR TRUNKS, LIKE A CHILD SUCKING ITS THUMB.

. . .

MALE ELEPHANTS BATTLE
EACH OTHER DURING
MATING TIME. SOMETIMES,
THEY EVEN FIGHT TO THE
DEATH. ONLY THE STRONGEST
MALES WILL GET TO MATE.

The inability to eat and chew food is a common cause of death, as few *predators* can kill an adult elephant. In fact, there is only one animal that poses a real threat to elephants: humans.

In Asia, elephants are captured and used to haul lumber through forests where there are no roads. A young elephant is paired with a young man for training, and the two might spend their whole lives working together. A fully trained elephant knows seventy to one hundred commands.

(OPPOSITE) WHEN IT IS TIME FOR AN ELEPHANT TO DIE, OTHER HERD MEMBERS STAY CLOSE BY TO COMFORT IT. AFTER IT IS GONE, THEY MAY STAY AND GUARD ITS BODY FOR HOURS. IT HAS EVEN BEEN SAID THAT ELEPHANTS VISIT THE BONES OF THEIR RELATIVES.

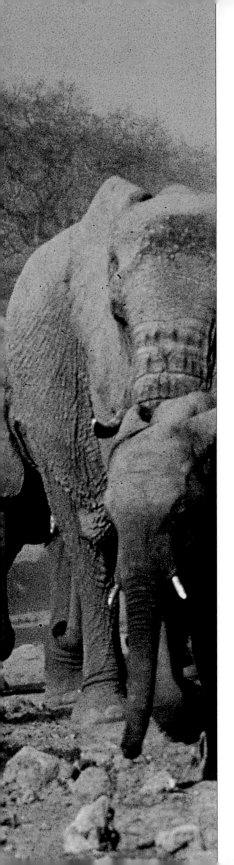

5
THE IVORY THREAT

A hundred years ago, 5 to 10 million elephants wandered freely across Africa. By 1970, there were just 3 million elephants left. Ten years later, there were only 1.3 million. By 1990, the number was cut in half again, to around 600,000. Many people feared there would soon be none left.

One reason so many elephants died is that they no longer had enough land on which to roam in search of food. Land that was once occupied by elephants and other

AN ELEPHANT HERD IN NAMIBIA NATIONAL PARK. THIS PARK HAS BEEN SET ASIDE ESPECIALLY FOR WILDLIFE, INCLUDING ELEPHANTS.

THESE TROPHIES ARE CARVED FROM IVORY. MANY ELEPHANTS HAVE LOST THEIR LIVES SO THAT CARVINGS SUCH AS THESE COULD BE MADE.

wild animals had been taken over by people for farm–ing and raising cattle. Even where parks had been set aside for them, they sometimes trampled everything to dust. With nowhere to go, the elephants starved.

Another more serious problem was hunting. Elephant tusks are made of smooth, hard ivory, which is very beautiful and easy to carve. The oldest known sculpture of a person was carved from mammoth ivory 26,000 years ago. Since then, people have carved ivory into everything from combs to pool balls to piano keys.

THESE ARE THE BONES OF AN ELEPHANT HUNTED ILLEGALLY. SINCE THE SALE OF IVORY HAS BEEN BANNED, SIGHTS LIKE THIS ARE BECOMING RARE.

As hunters had more and more powerful guns, it became easier for them to kill thousands of elephants just to chop off their tusks. They even killed elephants protected in wildlife reserves. There were always plenty of people willing to break the law and kill elephants when a single tusk was worth thousands of dollars.

IN 1989, 13 TONS OF IVORY WAS BURNED IN KENYA. THIS MASSIVE BONFIRE WAS A SIGN TO POACHERS THAT KENYA WOULD NO LONGER BUY THEIR IVORY.

By the 1980s, *poachers* were killing up to 100,000 elephants a year. Because older elephants had the biggest tusks, they were killed first, creating many orphans and leaderless groups. In some parks, elephants stopped trumpeting: they remembered that poachers had lured members of their herds with fake calls.

The only way to put an end to poaching was to ban the sale of ivory. In 1989, many countries, including the United States, made it a crime to trade ivory. The price of ivory quickly dropped from four hundred dollars per kilogram in 1989 to sixty dollars in the first year of the ban. By 1995 the price fell to three dollars. With

In 1988, two million Japanese bought pieces of ivory with their names carved in them to use as ink stamps. Thousands of elephants were slaughtered to meet the demand. The killing ended only with a ban on ivory sales.

AFRICAN ELEPHANTS NEED A LOT OF LAND TO SURVIVE. BUT PEOPLE IN AFRICA ALSO NEED LAND TO MAKE A LIVING. CONSERVATION GROUPS AND AFRICAN GOVERNMENTS ARE CREATING PROGRAMS THAT HELP AFRICANS MAKE MONEY FROM TOURISTS WHO COME TO SEE ELEPHANTS. THAT WAY, PEOPLE AND ELEPHANTS CAN SHARE THE LAND AND LIVE AS NEIGHBORS.

little money to be made from poaching, the slaughter mostly stopped. In 1997, however, three countries were allowed to sell old ivory, which some people fear will lead to more poaching.

Land for elephants remains a problem, too. In Asia, elephants live in the forests of Indonesia, Thailand, and other countries. But Asian forests are being cut down at an alarming rate, and fewer and fewer wild elephants have anywhere to live. A hundred years ago, 100,000 elephants lived in Asia. Now, there are fewer than 35,000.

The only way to save elephants and other creatures is to leave them enough wild land. During the upcoming century, as the number of people on Earth continues to grow, this will be one of our biggest challenges.

A MALE ELEPHANT GRAZING IN A MARSH IN TANZANIA. TO SAVE THE ELEPHANT, WE MUST SAVE THE LAND ON WHICH IT LIVES.

clone: to use a single cell from one animal to grow another animal that is exactly the same.

conservation: saving wild animals, plants, and habitats from destruction.

dugong: an animal, also called a sea cow, that lives in the water and is a distant relative of the elephant.

herbivore: an animal that eats only plants.

herd: a group of elephants or other animals that live together.

hyrax: a rabbit–sized animal that resembles a guinea pig.

ivory: the smooth, hard substance elephant tusks are made of.

mammal: the class of animals that includes elephants, humans, dogs, cats, mice, and thousands of other warm–blooded creatures that gives birth to live young who drink their mothers' milk.

poacher: someone who hunts animals illegally.

predator: an animal that hunts and kills other animals for food.

species: a group of animals with similar features that are able to reproduce.

trunk: the long, flexible, muscular nose of an elephant.

tusks: the two, long, pointed teeth jutting from an elephant's mouth.

woolly mammoth: a larger, hairier relative of the elephant that lived during the last ice age and died out 10,000 years ago.

BOOKS

Harman, Amanda and Rudolf Steiner. *Elephants.* Endangered series. Tarrytown, NY: Benchmark, 1996.

Krishnaswami, Uma. *The Broken Tusk: Stories of the Hindu God Ganesha.* New Haven: Linnet, 1996.

Levine, Stuart. *Elephants.* San Diego: Lucent, 1998.

Redmond, Ian. *Elephant.* Eyewitness Books series. NY: Knopf, 1993.

Redmond, Ian. *Elephants.* Wildlife at Risk series. NY: Bookwright, 1990.

Schmidt, Jeremy. *In the Village of the Elephants.* NY: Walker, 1994.

Smith, Roland and Michael J. Schmidt. *In the Forest with the Elephants.* San Diego, NY, London: Gulliver Books, Harcourt Brace, 1998.

WEBSITES

PBS (from the television show *Nature*)
www.pbs.org/wnet/nature/elephants/

Elephant Information Repository
http://elephant.elehost.com

Indolink (stories about Ganesha, the elephant–headed Hindu god)
www.indolink.com/Kidz/strGnesh.html

World Wildlife Fund—Endangered Species
www.worldwildlife.org (Search for "Endangered Species—Elephant")

Ruby, the painting elephant
www.phoenixzoo.org/news/ruby/

Martin Schwabacher grew up in Minneapolis, Minnesota, and has lived in Rhode Island, Texas, and New York City. He is the author of more than fifteen books for young people, including *Bears* in the Animals Animals series.

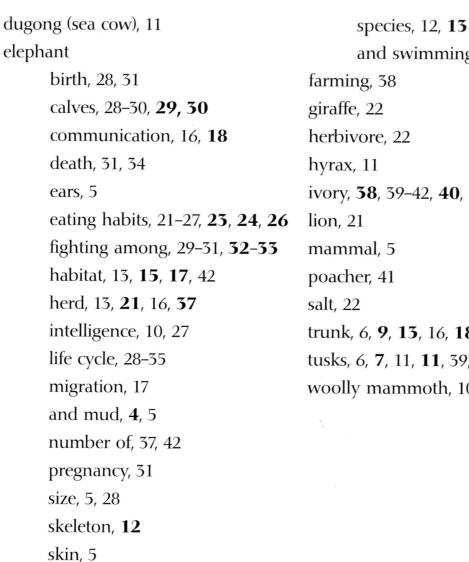

INDEX